It's My Body

Hair

Lola Schaefer

www.raintreepublishers.co.uk
Visit our website to find out more information about **Raintree** books.

To order:
☎ Phone 44 (0) 1865 888112
▤ Send a fax to 44 (0) 1865 314091
▢ Visit the Raintree Bookshop at **www.raintreepublishers.co.uk** to browse our catalogue and order online.

First published in Great Britain by Raintree, Halley Court, Jordan Hill, Oxford OX2 8EJ, part of Harcourt Education.
Raintree is a registered trademark of Harcourt Education Ltd.

Editorial: Jennifer Gillis and Diyan Leake
Design: Sue Emerson and Michelle Lisseter
Picture Research: Jennifer Gillis
Production: Lorraine Hicks

Originated by Dot Gradations
Printed and bound in China by South China Printing Company

ISBN 1 844 21648 9
07 06 05 04 03
10 9 8 7 6 5 4 3 2 1

British Library Cataloguing in Publication Data
Schaefer, Lola
Hair
612.7'99
A full catalogue record for this book is available from the British Library.

Acknowledgements
The publishers would like to thank the following for permission to reproduce photographs: Corbis pp. 4 (Larry Williams), 5 (Ariel Skelly), 9 (Rold Bruderer); Heinemann Library pp. 6 (Janet Moran), 7 (Brian Warling), 10 (Brian Warling), 11 (Brian Warling), 14 (Greg Williams), 15 (Gareth Boden), 17 (Robert Lifson), 18 (Brian Warling), 19 (Robert Lifson), 20 (Brian Warling), 21 (Brian Warling), 22 (Brian Warling), 23 (Brian Warling), 24 (Brian Warling), back cover (eyebrows, Brian Warling); PhotoEdit (David Young-Wolff) p. 8; PictureQuest (Chris Arend/Alaska Stock Images) p. 16; Science Photo Library pp. 12 (Sheila Terry), 13 (David Scharf), 23 (follicle, David Scharf), back cover (follicle, David Scharf).

Cover photograph reproduced with permission of Getty Image/Taxi.

Every effort has been made to contact copyright holders of any material reproduced in this book. Any omissions will be rectified in subsequent printings if notice is given to the publishers.

Some words are shown in bold, **like this**. You can find them in the glossary on page 23.

Contents

What is my hair?

Your hair is part of your body.

Your body is made up of
many parts.

Each part of your body does a job.

Your hair helps keep you warm.

Where does hair grow?

Hair grows on people's heads.

Fine hair grows all over your body.

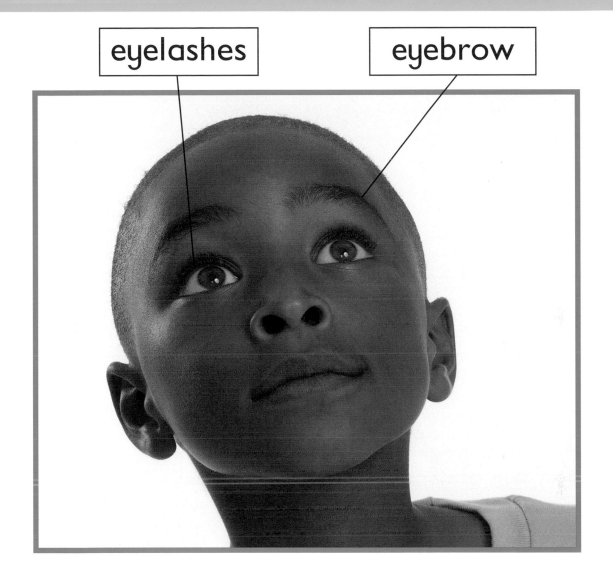

eyelashes

eyebrow

Hair grows on your face.

Eyelashes and **eyebrows** are made of hair.

What does hair look like?

Hair can be black, brown, yellow or red.

Some hair is grey or white.

Hair can be curly or straight.

It can be short or long.

What does hair feel like?

Some hair feels smooth and soft.

Hair can be thick or thin.

Hair can feel fuzzy.

It can feel prickly.

How does hair grow?

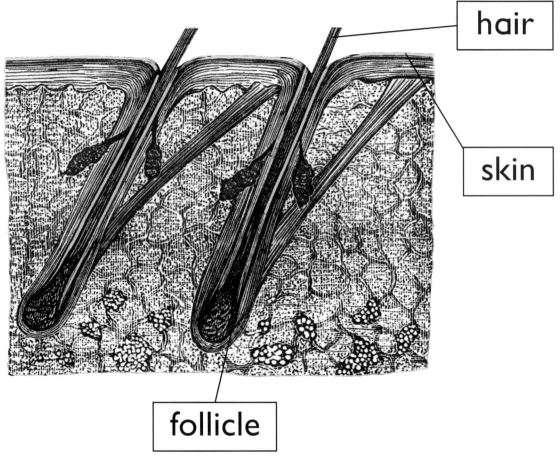

hair

skin

follicle

Pictures can make little things look big.

This drawing shows how hair starts in the **follicle**.

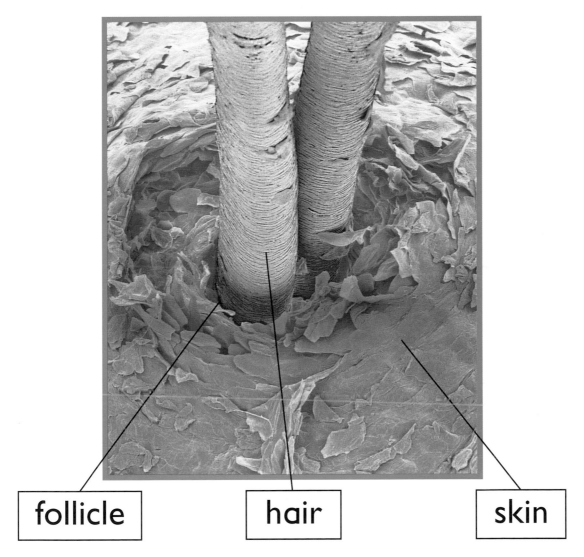

| follicle | hair | skin |

This picture is a photograph showing hair growing out of the skin.

What does hair do?

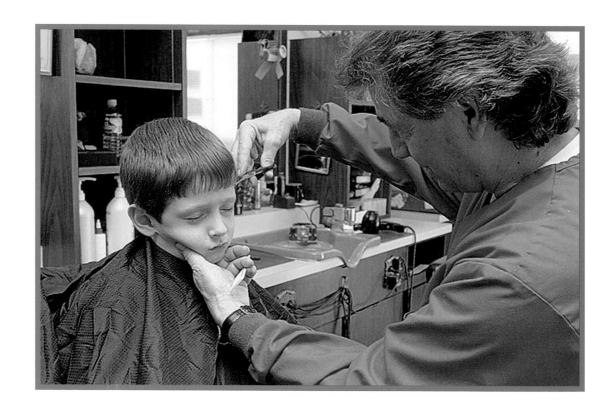

Your hair grows and grows.

If you didn't cut it, it would get very long.

Hair falls out when it stops growing.

New hair grows to take its place.

What is hair for?

Some hair keeps parts of your body safe.

Hair can keep snow off people's faces.

Hair helps keep your head safe
from the sun.

What are eyebrows for?

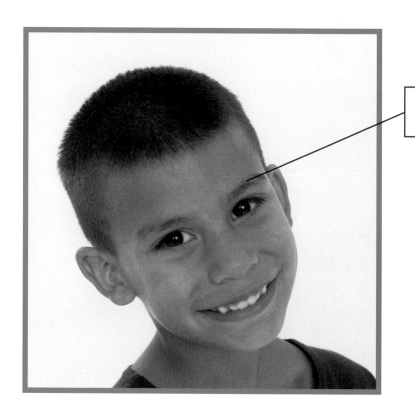

eyebrow

Your **eyebrows** help keep your eyes safe.

Eyebrows keep things out of your eyes.

Eyebrows can keep sweat out of your eyes.

They can keep dirt out of your eyes, too.

What are eyelashes for?

eyelashes

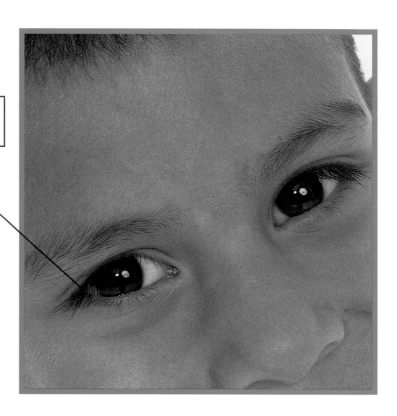

Eyelashes help keep your eyes safe.

You have many eyelashes all around your eyes.

Eyelashes clean the air when you blink.

They sweep the dust away from your eyes.

Quiz

Do you know what these are?

Look for the answers on page 24.

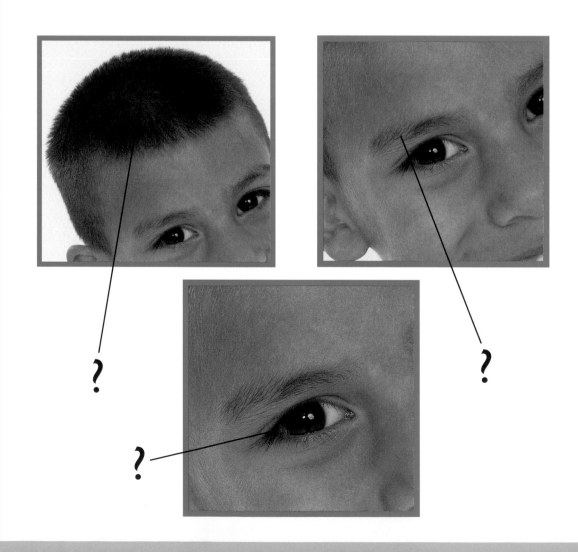

?

?

?

Glossary

eyebrows
the hairs on your forehead just above each eye

eyelashes
the hairs growing on the edge of each eyelid

follicle
tiny hole in the skin where hair grows out

Index

Answers to quiz on page 22

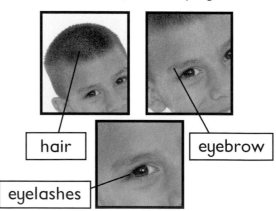

hair

eyebrow

eyelashes

Titles in the It's My Body series include:

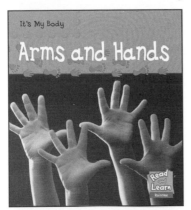

Hardback   1 844 21647 0

Hardback   1 844 21648 9

Hardback   1 844 21649 7

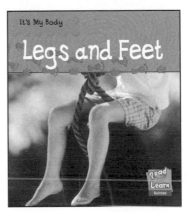

Hardback   1 844 21650 0

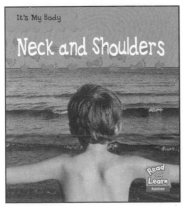

Hardback   1 844 21651 9

Find out about the other titles in this series on our website www.raintreepublishers.co.uk